MW01078055

The Memorial Hall
of the Victims in Nanjing Massacre by Japanese Invaders

The Memorial Hall
of the Victims in Nanjing Massacre
by Japanese Invaders

The Memorial Hall of the Victims in Nanjing Massacre by Japanese Invaders
In collaboration with London Editions (HK) Ltd

Contents

Inaugurated on 15 August 1985, the Memorial Hall of the Victims in Nanjing Massacre by Japanese Invaders (called the 'Memorial Hall') is located in the south-western corner of Nanjing known as Jiangdongmen, which was the site of the massacre and the site of the 'Mass Grave of Ten Thousand Corpses'. Expanded and enlarged, respectively, from 1994 to 1995 and from 2005 to 2007, the Memorial Hall was opened to the public on 13 December 2007, marking the 70th anniversary of the 300,000 victims of the Nanjing Massacre.

Located on Shuiximen Street, the Memorial Hall covers a total area of 74,000 square metres, with a floor area of 25,000 square metres and an exhibition area of 12,000 square metres. As a site-based museum of history, the Memorial Hall consists of four functional sections, namely the Exhibition and Meeting Centre, the Centre for the Memory of the Victims of the Massacre, the Peace Park and the Administrative Area.

The exhibitions in the Memorial Hall fall into four categories: the permanent exhibition, themed exhibits, the exhibit on the site of the 'Mass Grave of Ten Thousand Corpses' and temporary exhibitions. The regular exhibition, *A Human Holocaust – An Exhibition of the Historical Facts of the Nanjing Massacre Perpetrated by the Japanese Invaders* aims at unfolding an authentic chapter of history through numerous cultural relics and valuable archives, which are supplemented by simple and unsophisticated artistic forms, thus tugging at visitors' heartstrings. The Memorial Hall has collected more than 150,000 articles to underpin its display and exhibits, including 25,000 cultural relics, among them 315 recognized as Grade 1, 672 Grade 2 and 965 Grade 3.

Designed by Qi Kang and He Jingtang, two master architects in China, the spatial layout of the expanded Memorial Hall, in the shape of an 'Ark of Peace', implies the 'turning of swords into ploughshares', rendering an air of solemnity and stateliness. The Memorial Hall conveys the symbolic significance of 'Death and Peace', as evidenced by 'the Bones of the Killed and the Ruins of the Destroyed' on one hand and 'Home for the Humanity and Peace for the World' on the other hand.

The Memorial Hall has about 30 sculptures, including, on the Sculpture Square: *A Ruined Family, The Refugees, The Cry of Wronged Souls, Call of the Mother, Goddess of Peace*, and a large group sculpture Catastrophe of the Ancient City. These sculpture installations form critical links with the exhibitions outside the Memorial Hall, between the square, the monuments, and other displays, expanding the spatial layout and enhancing the quality of the exhibits in the Memorial Hall.

The past 25 years have witnessed the tremendous achievements that the Memorial Hall has made in terms of presentation and exhibition, academic study and training, public education, exchange and co-operation. The Memorial Hall has so far received over 30 million visitors, and, since the opening of the new hall, five million annually. In addition, exhibitions on the Nanjing Massacre have been organized in more than 10 countries and regions including Japan, the Philippines, the USA and Denmark. Tour exhibitions have been held in over 20 Chinese cities, including Beijing, Wuhan, Shenyang and Guangzhou, and more than 200 special exhibitions and events visited by over 1.5 million visitors in total, for example 'Commemoration for the Compatriots Killed in the Nanjing Massacre – Nanjing International Peace Assembly', have been organized. In addition, the Memorial Hall has forged friendly and co-operative relations with its 10 counterparts worldwide, including Auschwitz–Birkenau State Museum; Museum of the Great Patriotic War, Moscow; Le Mémorial de Caen – Cité de l'Histoire pour la Paix; and the Kyoto Museum for World Peace, Ritsumeikan University.

Since its opening, the new Memorial Hall has been showered with praise for its splendid exhibitions, magnificent architecture and elegant sculptures from visitors both at home and abroad. As a result, the new Memorial Hall has been selected into the World Top 10 Dark Tourist Destinations, China's Grade 1 Museums and State-Protected Historic Sites, and has won many major prizes, including China's Top 10 Exhibitions, the Luban Prize for architectural projects and the Prize for Achievement in Urban Sculpture in New China.

The Memorial Hall of the Victims in Nanjing Massacre by Japanese Invaders

Part I. **The Hall of Testimony**

Covering an area of some 5,000 square metres, *A Human Holocaust – An Exhibition of the Historical Facts of the Nanjing Massacre Perpetrated by the Japanese Invaders* consists of 11 units, with over 3,500 photos, 3,000 cultural relics and 140 historical videos on display. Through the testimonies of a large number of witnesses, physical and written evidence, audios and videos, and archives on historical events, the Exhibition highlights the authenticity of the Nanjing Massacre. As for the spatial layout and design, cultural relics, photos and academic findings have been integrated with versatile displays to remarkable effect.

Photos in the Display Space

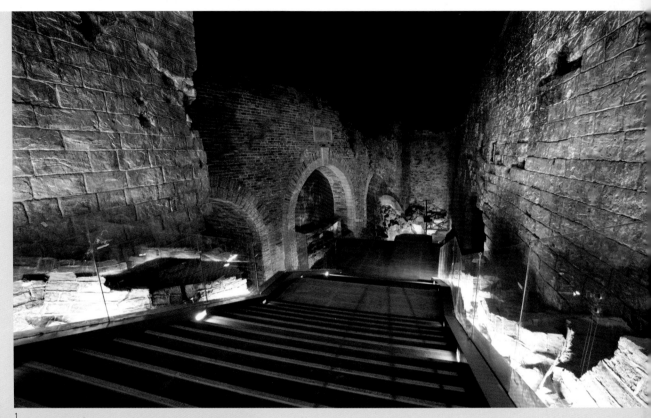

1 Central Hall: Nanjing at War
2 Entrance to the Exhibition
3 Victims 300,000: *Wall Bearing the Names of the 300,000*
4 *Victims of the Nanjing Massacre*

3

4

1

2

3

The Memorial Hall of the Victims in Nanjing Massacre by Japanese Invaders

1 *The Fierce Battle at Guanghuamen* (Diorama)
2 The Situation in China before the Fall of Nanjing
3 *The Streets in Nanjing after the Japanese Air Raids* (Diorama)
4 The actual remains of the victims unearthed during the third excavation are kept in the Exhibition Hall of Historical Records.
5 *Massacre*

1

2　　　　　　　　　3　　　　　　　　　4

5

1 *Slaughter, Life, Buddha – Nanjing Massacre*
   (oil painting)
2 *Sporadic Slaughter*
3 *Rape and Ravage*
4 *Rape and Ravage*
5 *The Unsafe Safety Zone*

1

前事不忘 后事之师

2

3

The Memorial Hall of the Victims in Nanjing Massacre by Japanese Invaders

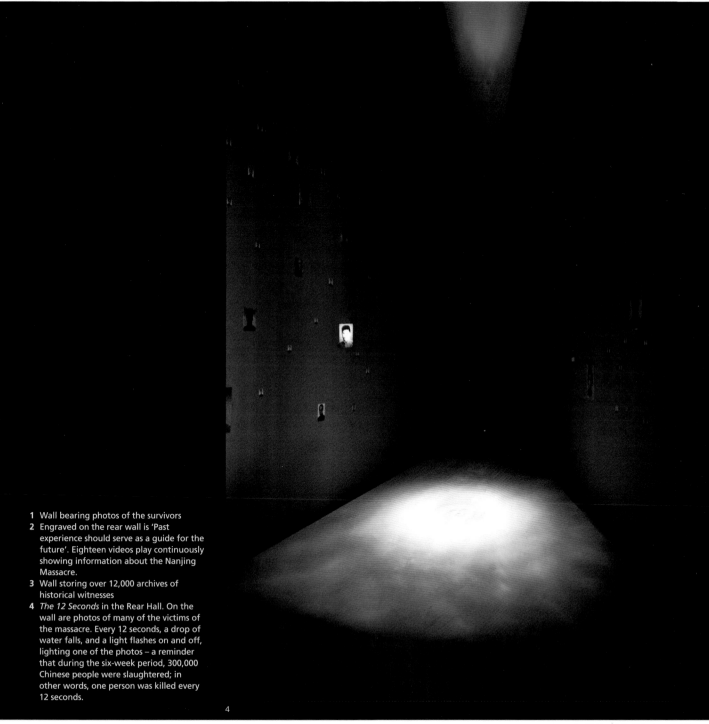

1 Wall bearing photos of the survivors
2 Engraved on the rear wall is 'Past experience should serve as a guide for the future'. Eighteen videos play continuously showing information about the Nanjing Massacre.
3 Wall storing over 12,000 archives of historical witnesses
4 *The 12 Seconds* in the Rear Hall. On the wall are photos of many of the victims of the massacre. Every 12 seconds, a drop of water falls, and a light flashes on and off, lighting one of the photos – a reminder that during the six-week period, 300,000 Chinese people were slaughtered; in other words, one person was killed every 12 seconds.

4

1 In 1927, the Republic of China made Nanjing its capital. Covering an area of 476 square kilometres and with a population of 1.01 million, Nanjing saw its rapid development into a hustling and bustling metropolis in 1937. The photo shows Xinjiekou Square before the War of Resistance against Japanese Aggression (1937–1945)
Excerpt from *Old Nanking*

2 On 15 August 1937, the Imperial Japanese Navy Air Squadron made its first cross-ocean bombardment on Nanjing
Excerpt from *Japanese–Chinese War* [Japan]

3 On 13 December 1937 the Japanese army occupied Nanjing
The picture shows the Japanese army seizing the National Government building
Excerpt from *Photos of the Japanese War in Nanjing* [Japan]

4 An old woman being led by a man to take refuge from the calamity
Excerpt from *A Record of the Atrocities of the Japanese Invaders*

5 On 17 December 1937, the Japanese army conducted an 'Entering-the-City Ceremony'
Excerpt from *Asahi Graph* [Japan]

6

6 The corpses of the captured Chinese who were shot dead *en masse* by the Japanese soldiers piled up on top of each other
Preserved by Luo Jin and Wu Xuan and collected in the Second Historical Archives of China
7 The Japanese army searched for and arrested young Chinese in Nanjing
Excerpt from *Mainichi Shimbu – Hizo Fukyoka Shashin* (Banned Photos) [Japan]
8 The corpses of the Chinese slaughtered by the Japanese soldiers heaped up on the bank of the Yangtze River
Excerpt from *Murase Moriyasu – Watashino Jyugun Cyugoku-sensen* (My China Front) [Japan]

5

7

8

1

2

1 The Japanese soldiers killed the Chinese, piling firewood and pouring gasoline on the corpses to burn them
Excerpt from *Murase Moriyasu – Watashino Jyugun Cyugoku-sensen* (My China Front) [Japan]

2 A farmer killed by the Japanese soldiers on the outskirts of Nanjing
Excerpt from *A Record of the Atrocities of the Japanese Invaders*

3 A three-year-old baby in Nanjing was shot dead by a Japanese soldier
Excerpt from *A Record of the Atrocities of the Japanese Invaders*

4 The Japanese soldiers killed Chinese civilians with their sabres
Excerpt from An Album of Photos of the Japanese Massacre in Nanjing

5 The 'Pond of Blood': Unarmed Chinese officers and soldiers on the outskirts of Nanjing, hands tied behind their back, were shot dead and then thrown into the pond by the Japanese soldiers. About 300 corpses were found in the pond.
Excerpt from *A Record of the Atrocities of the Japanese Invaders*

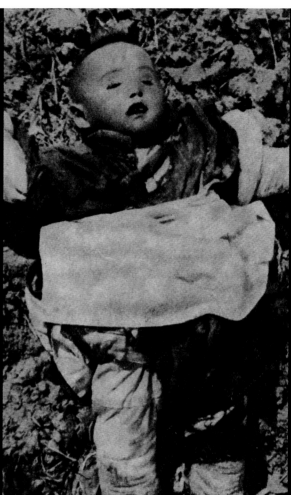

3

4

5

百人斬り"超記録"
向井106─105野田
両少尉さらに延長戦

"百人斬り競争"の両將校
（右）野田巖少尉（左）向井敏明少尉
＝常州にて佐藤（振）特派員撮影＝

【紫金山麓にて十二日淺海、鈴木兩特派員發】南京入りまで〃百人斬り競争〃といふ競争をはじめた例の片桐部隊の勇士向井敏明、野田巖兩少尉は十日の紫金山攻略戰のときさらに百六對百五といふレコードを作つて十日正午兩少尉はさすがに刃こぼれした日本刀を片手に對面した

野田「おいおれは百五だが貴様は」と笑さう、だが故めて百五十人中の向井少尉が「百人斬りドンゲーム」の競争を識つてのち知らぬうちに兩方で百人を超えてゐたのは愉快ぢや、俺の關孫六が双こぼれしたのは一人を鐡兜もろともに唐竹割にしたからだ

向井「アハハハ」總じていつまで十一日からいよいよ百五十人斬りはじまつた、十一日霧中山陵を眼下に見下す紫金山で蛇髪長狩濱最後」向井「おれは百六だ！」──兩少尉は「どうちや」と怒り意見一致して少尉は「アハハ」總じいつ〃れが先きに百人斬つたかにいづれが先きに百人斬つたかにいつれは不問、結局「ちやドロンゲーこれは不問

ちや、戰ひ濟んだらこの日本刀は貴社に寄贈すると約束したよ十一日の午前三時友軍の珍戰術紫金山淺敵あぶり出しには俺もあぶり出されて彈雨の中を「えいますよ」と刀をかついで棒立ちになつてゐたが一つもあたらわさこれもこの孫六のおかげだと飛來する敵彈の中で百六の生血を飛つた孫六を記者に示した

1 On 14 December 1937, the *Tokyo Nichi Nichi Shimbun* carried a series of reports by Asami Kazuo and Suzuki Jiro on the 'Contest to kill 100 Chinese using a sword between Noda Tsuyoshi and Mukai Toshiaki' at the foot of Purple Mountain. By that time, Mukai Toshiaki had slaughtered 105 Chinese and Noda Tsuyoshi 106. Their failure to judge who had first killed 100 people pitted them against each other in 'extra innings' for a new aim of 150 kills.

2 This photo, seized from a captured Japanese soldier, laid bare the barbarities committed by the Japanese soldiers in amusing themselves by slaughtering civilians.
Excerpt from *A Record of the Atrocities of the Japanese Invaders*

2

1 A very sick 16-year-old girl, having been gang-raped by the Japanese soldiers
Excerpt from *A Record of the Atrocities of the Japanese Invaders*

2 Having been gang-raped, this woman was coerced into undressing herself to entertain the Japanese soldiers. This photo was seized from a captured Japanese soldier.
Excerpt from *A Record of the Atrocities of the Japanese Invaders*

3 This photo, seized from a Japanese soldier, shows an old woman, in extreme agony, being undressed and raped by a Japanese soldier
Excerpt from *An Album of Paintings on the Anti-Japanese War and the Establishment of New China*

4 After being raped by the Japanese soldiers, this pregnant woman was ripped open at her stomach, and left with her bowels exposed
Excerpt from *An Album of Photos of the Japanese Massacre in Nanjing*

5 In December 1937, Japanese soldiers plundered the possessions of Nanjing residents and carried them away on Zhongshan Road by various means of transportation including trucks, carriages, bicycles and prams. The news censorship department of the Japanese Military refused to allow this photo to be released because it exposed the atrocities of the Japanese soldiers.
Excerpt from *Mainichi Shimbu – Hizo Fukyoka Shashin* (Banned Photos) [Japan]

6 The surrounding area of Hanzhongmen in Nanjing was in ruins
Photographed by Christian Kroeger [Germany]

7 The city walls at Zhongshanmen Gate were demolished by Japanese gunfire
Excerpt from *Murase Moriyasu – Watashino Jyugun Cyugoku-sensen* (My China Front) [Japan]

5

6

7

3

1

2

1　In November 1937, some westerners staying in Nanjing decided to establish an international relief agency entitled 'The International Committee for the Nanking Safety Zone' in the hope that it would serve as a shelter for refugees. John H. D. Rabe from Siemens AG China Corporation was selected as Chairman of the Committee. Covering an area of 3.86 square kilometres, the Safety Zone, or the Refugee Zone, was located in north-western Nanjing with highways on four sides. Twenty-five refugee camps were set up in the Zone, accommodating as many as 250,000 refugees.

2　Children taking refuge at the University of Nanjing
Photo from the collection of the Yale University Divinity School Library

3　On 16 December 1937, Japanese soldiers captured Chinese soldiers on Zhongshan Road
Excerpt from *Aggression by the Japanese Army: China and Korea*

4　Sixty-seven-year-old Eva Heinz was looking after the orphans due to the war turmoil
Excerpt from *One Hundred Days in the Nanking Safety Zone* [Japan]

5　Japanese troops searched for and arrested young Chinese inside the Safety Zone. This wall in the Safety Zone seemed to be a demarcation line between life and death for the refugees.
Excerpt from *The Great Nanjing Massacre: Photos and Evidence*

6　For the sake of safety, a group of women refugees moved from one camp to another
Photo taken by John Magee [USA]

7　A 14-year-old child whose right leg was injured by a Japanese soldier was receiving medical treatment at Nanjing Drum Tower Hospital
Excerpt from *A Record of the Atrocities of the Japanese Invaders*

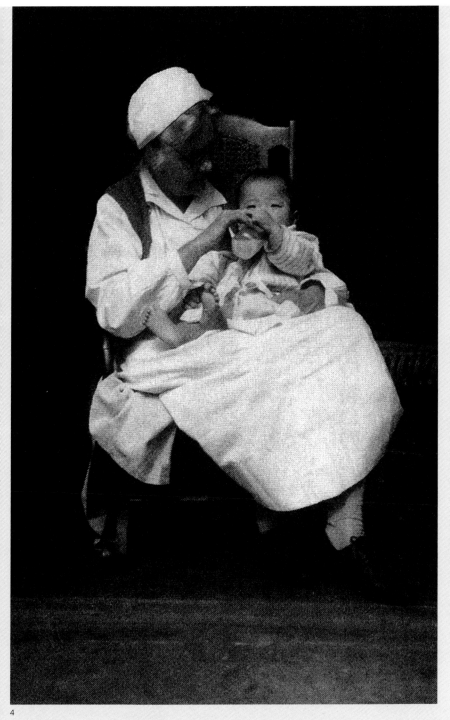

4

5

6

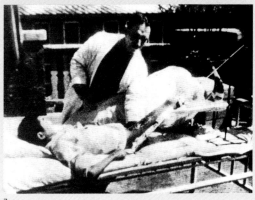

7

1

2

1 The interior of the International Military Tribunal for the Far East
   The Military Tribunal brought an indictment against Japanese war criminals on 29 April 1946, put them on
   trial on 3 May and passed judgment on them on 4 November 1948.
   Photo from the collection of the United States National Archives and Records Administration
2 Tani Hisao, a principal war criminal, was put on trial at the Nanjing War Crimes Tribunal
   Photo from the collection of the Second Historical Archives of China

3 Relics

1

2

3

1 Risking his life, Rev. John Magee from the USA shot scenes of the Nanjing Massacre on site with his 16-mm movie camera. George Fitch, Director-General of the International Safety Zone, took the film to the Kodak office in Shanghai, where four copies were made and sent to the appropriate people in Germany, France, Japan and the USA.
   The photo shows the movie camera and original film footage donated by John Magee's son to the Memorial Hall on 2 October 2002.
2 In December 1937, Mrs Guo, a Nanjing resident, searched the site of the mass massacre on the riverside in Xiaguan District for her son Guo Xueli, who had fled by crossing the river. The iron barrel she picked up bore the words 'Osaka Co. Ltd, Miyazaki Store, produced in Showa of 12 (1937)'. Still half full of gasoline, the barrel had been used by the Japanese troops for burning Chinese corpses.
3 As a solider of the 16th Division of the Imperial Japanese Army, Azuma Shirou was engaged in the Nanjing Massacre. In order to express his remorse and atone for his war crimes, he had his wartime diary *The Diary of Azuma Shirou* published openly in Japan. On 7 March 1998, he donated his diaries to the Memorial Hall.

4

1 In January 1939, Gao Guanwu, Supervisor of the puppet Nanking Municipal Administration, inscribed 'Tombstone With No Master' on a tablet. This is a rubbing of it, which translates roughly as follows: By October 1938, remains had been found at the city gate, in the forest, on the mountain and by the streams. I collected these remains, 26 in total, and buried them. Two months later, a villager reported to me that there were a large number of abandoned corpses at Maoshan, Maqun, Ma'an and Linggu Temple. At my order, the Bureau of Health sent men to collect the corpses. Around 3,000 in total, all of them were buried to the east of Linggu Temple. Photo from the collection of the Nanjing Archives

2 The remains of the victims unearthed at the 'Mass Grave of Ten Thousand Corpses' during the 1983–84 excavation at the site of the Nanjing Massacre at Jiangdongmen.

3 Beer bottles that had been used by the Japanese troops as well as the soles of shoes, buttons and other relics of the victims were found during the 1983–84 excavations at the 'Mass Grave of Ten Thousand Corpses' of the Nanjing Massacre at Jiangdongmen.

4 Between April 1998 and December 1999 the remains of more victims were discovered at Jiangdongmen. Covering an area of 170 square metres, the remains were piled up in seven layers, with a total of 208 corpses being found.

5 In 2006, a new mass grave for the remains of the victims was identified.

5

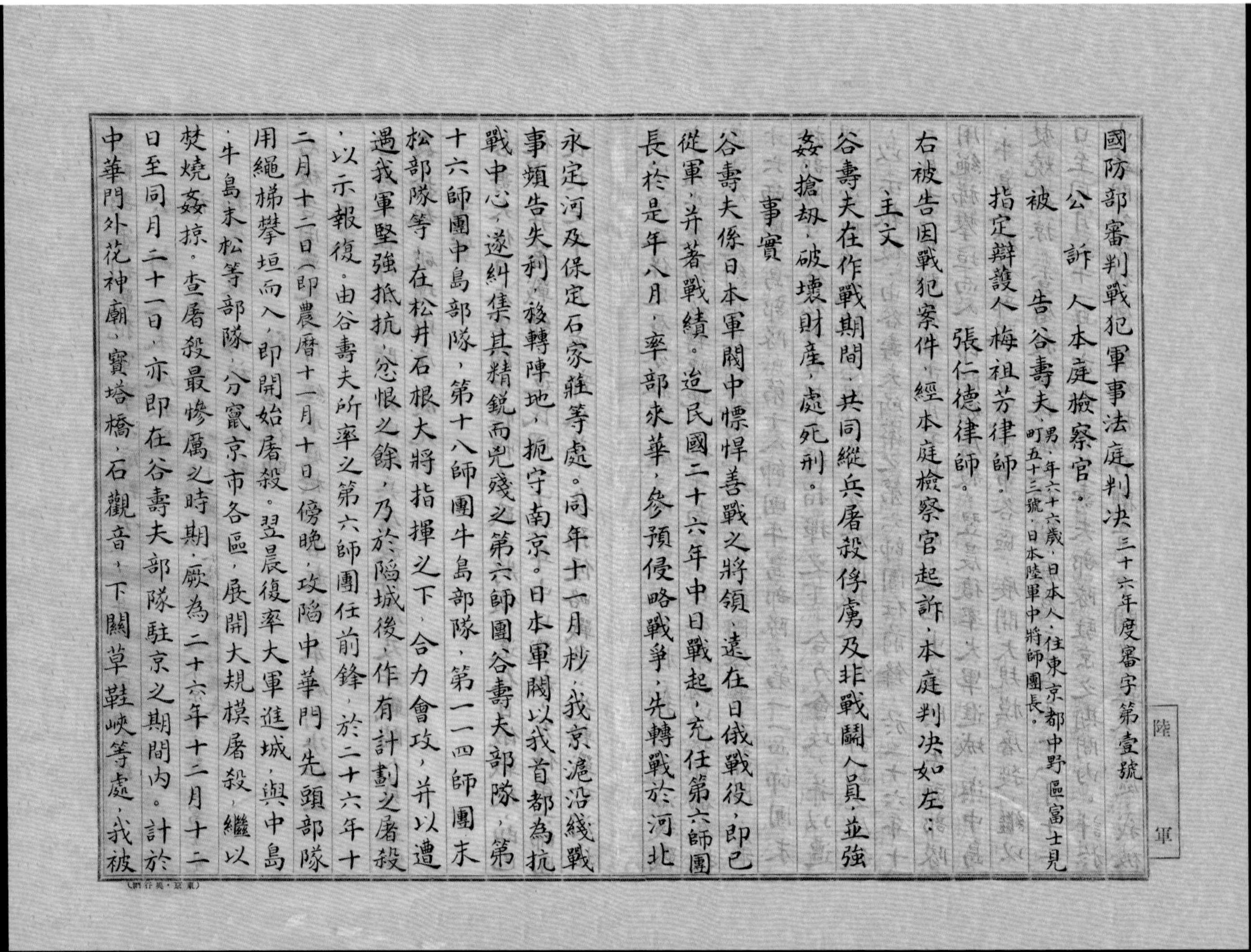

國防部審判戰犯軍事法庭判決三十六年度審字第壹號

陸軍

公訴人本庭檢察官。

被告谷壽夫，男，年六十六歲，日本人，住東京都中野區富士見町五十三號，日本陸軍中將師團長。

指定辯護人梅祖芳律師。

張仁德律師。

右被告因戰犯案件，經本庭檢察官起訴，本庭判決如左：

主文

谷壽夫在作戰期間，共同縱兵屠殺俘虜及非戰鬥人員，並強姦、搶劫、破壞財產，處死刑。

事實

谷壽夫係日本軍閥中慓悍善戰之將領，遠在日俄戰役，即已從軍，并著戰績。迨民國二十六年中日戰起，充任第六師團長。於是年八月，率部來華，參預侵略戰爭，先轉戰於河北、永定河及保定石家莊等處。同年十一月秒，我京滬沿綫戰事頻告失利，移轉陣地，扼守南京。日本軍閥以我首都為抗戰中心，遂糾集其精銳而凶殘之第六師團谷壽夫部隊，第十六師團中島部隊，第十八師團團牛島部隊，第一一四師團末松部隊等，在松井石根大將指揮之下，合力會攻，并以遭遇我軍堅強抵抗，忿恨之餘，乃於陷城後，作有計劃之屠殺，以示報復。由谷壽夫所率之第六師團任前鋒，於二十六年十二月十二日（即農曆十一月十日）傍晚，攻陷中華門，先頭部隊用繩梯攀垣而入，即開始屠殺。翌晨復率大軍進城，與中島、牛島、末松等部隊，分竄京市各區，展開大規模屠殺，繼以焚燒姦掠。查屠殺最慘屬之時期，厥為二十六年十二月十二日至同月二十一日，亦即在谷壽夫部隊駐京之期間內。計於中華門外花神廟、寶塔橋、石觀音、下關草鞋峽等處，我被

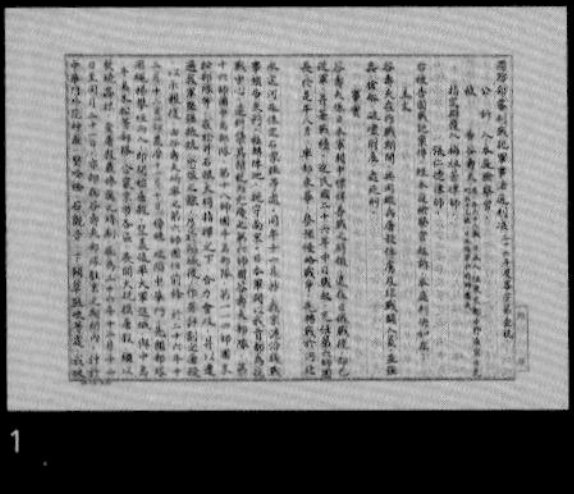

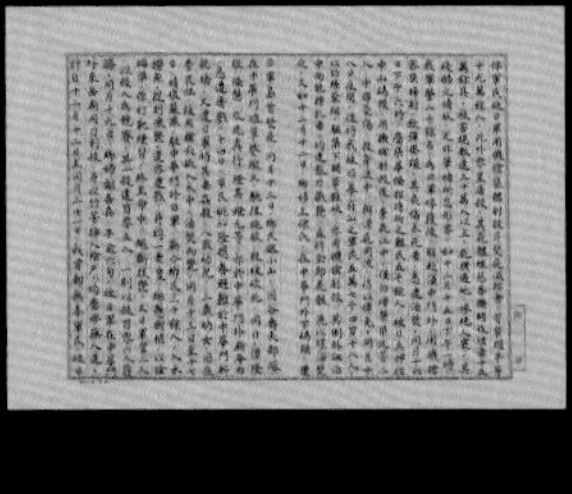

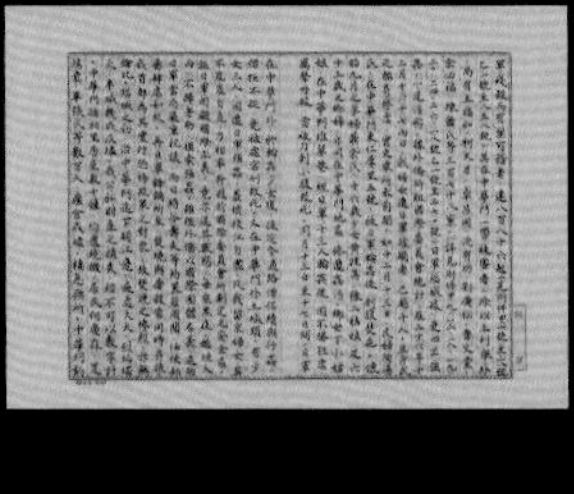

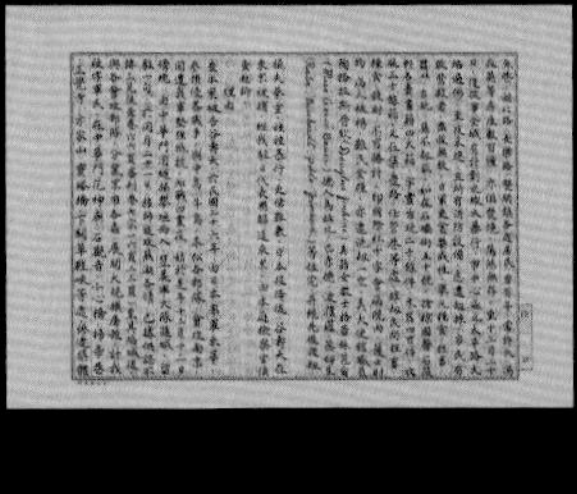

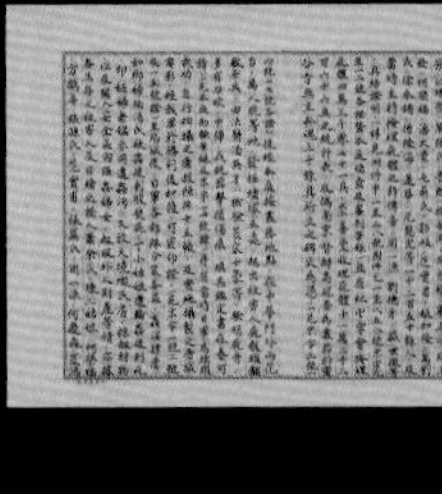

《取谷萬·京紀》

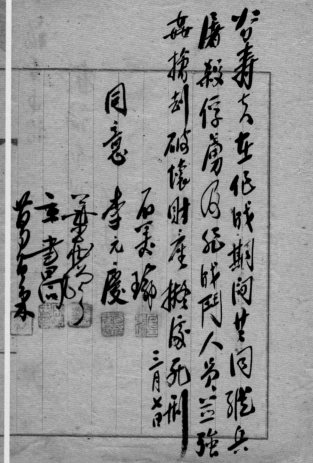

谷壽夫在作戰期間共同縱兵
屠殺俘虜及非戰鬥人員三萬
姦擄刼燒毀損財產擬處死刑

同意 李元慶 三月X日

石美瑜

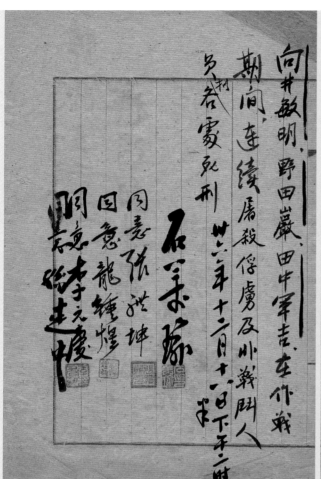

向井敏明、野田巖、田中軍吉在作戰
期間連續屠殺俘虜及非戰鬥人
員判各處死刑　卅二年十二月十八日下午二時

石美瑜

同意 張琮坤
同意 龍鍾煌
同意 李元慶
同志 從建中

2

1　The court verdict for war criminal Tani Hisao
2　The judgment sentencing Tani Hisao to death by the Nanjing War Crimes Tribunal

1

2

1 Light and heavy machine guns used by the Japanese troops in their occupation of Nanjing
2 Armaments and ammunition used by the Japanese troops in their invasion of China, including 88-calibre
shells, a 98-calibre field gun, grenade discharger, 97-calibre grenade, 38-calibre rifle and sabre.

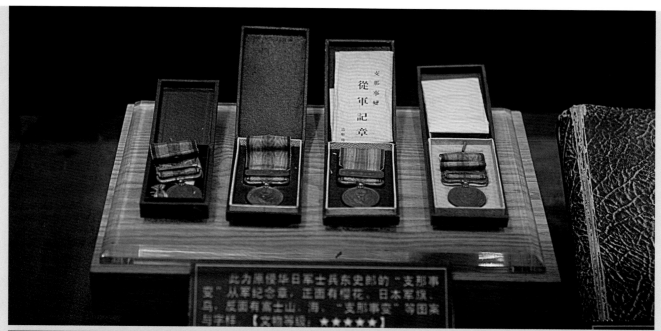

1 A souvenir badge of the 'China Incident' for Soldier Shiro Azuma
2 The bunker set up by the Chinese Army against the Japanese Aggression in 1937 (originally at Tangshan in the eastern suburb of Nanjing)

2

1

2

3

4

1 Tourist Centre
2 Visitors' Lounge
3 Historical records of the Nanjing Massacre in the Memorial Hall
4 The Memorial Hall guides

1

The Memorial Hall of the Victims in Nanjing Massacre by Japanese Invaders

Symbolizing an 'Ark of Peace', the Memorial Hall consists of the following sections: the Assembly Square composed of the *Wall of Calamity*, the Cenotaph and the *Bell of Peace*; the Exhibition Hall of Historical Records; the Memorial Square inscribed with the name of the Memorial Hall by Deng Xiaoping; the exquisite Graveyard Square, including the solemn Grave of the Remains of the Victims and the solemn site of the 'Mass Grave of Ten thousand Corpses'; the imposing Sacrificial Square; the serene Meditation Hall; and the Peace Park brimming with vitality.

In line with the geographical and geological characteristics of the Site of the Mass Massacre at Jiangdongmen, the Memorial Hall, as a masterpiece among commemorative buildings in China, features a perfect integration of natural environment, historical context and architectural structure in the form of squares, graveyards and tomb passages to interpret the themes of 'Life and Death' and 'Grief and Indignation'.

The construction of the colossal architectural installation was done in three stages. The Phase I & II Projects were designed by Qi Kang, Academician of the Chinese Academy of Sciences and Director of the Architectural Design & Research Institute of Southeast University; the Phase III Project was designed by He Jingtang, Academician of the Chinese Academy of Engineering and Dean of the School of Architecture of South China University of Technology. Their concerted efforts have given birth to this heart-stirring commemorative building.

2   3

1 The *Wall of Calamity*
2 Qi Kang
3 He Jingtang

The Memorial Hall

The Memorial Hall is like an 'Ark of Peace' rising high above the ground, in the shape of a ship's bow built up from a series of steps. It bears similarity to a broken military sword in profile; seen from above, it bears a resemblance to a sword turned into a ploughshare. While expressing the theme of 'Grief and Indignation', the architectural installation in its entirety, as a new landmark in Nanjing, conveys the significance of 'Peace'.

The Assembly Square 2

Paved with dark stones, the Assembly Square seems devoid of life. On the Square stands the *Wall of Calamity* fashioned out of black marble and carved with the words 'Victims 300,000' in 12 languages including Chinese, English, Japanese, Korean and Spanish.

1 View showing the Assembly Square in the distance
2 Bell of Peace

3 The Exhibition Hall of Historical Records

Situated inside the bow of the 'Ark of Peace', the Exhibition Hall of Historical Records is faced with black marble, lending an air of elegance and reverence. The exit – a long and narrow space created by the façade on one side and the oblique plan on the other – is deliberately claustrophobic.

Above: The Entrance to the Exhibition Hall of Historical Records **Bottom:** The Exit of the Exhibition Hall of Historical Records

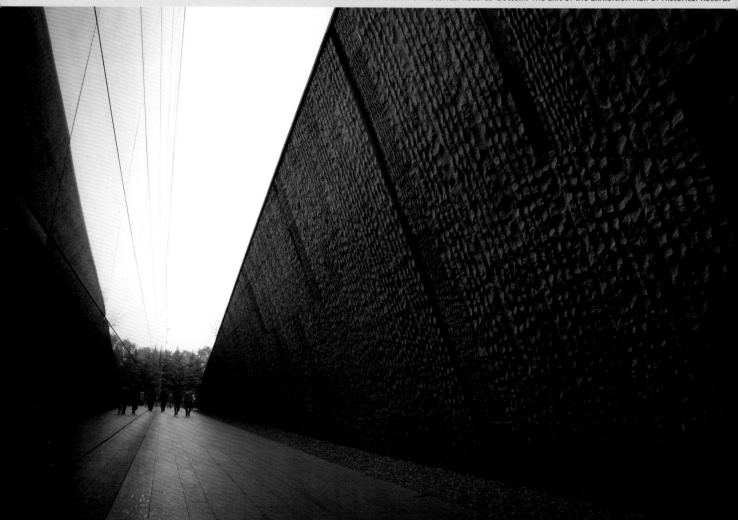

The Memorial Square

4

The grey stone wall bears the name of the Memorial Hall inscribed by Deng Xiaoping. The parapet on the right side is inscribed with the words – 'Victims 300,000' in Chinese, English and Japanese.

5 The Graveyard Square

The architectural complex here is designed as a memorial graveyard. Paved with pebble stones, this grassless square signifies piles of remains and death; the thriving lawn on both sides and evergreen trees outside the wall symbolize vitality and a fighting spirit. Such a stark contrast implies that there is a thin line between life and death. Several withered trees not only represent the destroyed buildings, one-third of all the buildings in Nanjing, but also suggest a melancholic atmosphere. In the yard of the site are withered trees, pebble stones and broken walls, three sets of large reliefs inlaid in the wall – *Calamity*, *Massacre* and *Memorial*, 17 monuments to the victims, a sculpture *Call of the Mother*, the *Wall Bearing the Names of the Victims of the Nanjing Massacre*, the Grave for the Remains of the Victims and the site of the 'Mass Grave of Ten Thousand Corpses'. All these constitute Graveyard Square, presenting a picture of horror and terror.

1

2

1 The site of the Grave for the Remains of the Victims
It is in this greenish-grey building that the remains of the victims are housed. In this sense, the bitterest theme is made clear in the simplest manner.
2 The site of the 'Mass Grave of Ten Thousand Corpses'

Pebble stones representing the
remains of the victims

6 The Sacrificial Square

In front of the black granite wall there burns an everlasting fire in memory of the immortality of the victims of the Nanjing Massacre. The Square is flanked by jagged monuments, without inscriptions, symbolizing the loss of life.

1

1 The Sacrificial Square
2 Everlasting Fire
3 The jagged monuments without inscriptions

2

3

7 The Meditation Hall

Faced with granite on both sides, the Meditation Hall houses a shallow pool. Flickering candlelight reflects a dark wall in the water, an image of mourning and contemplation.

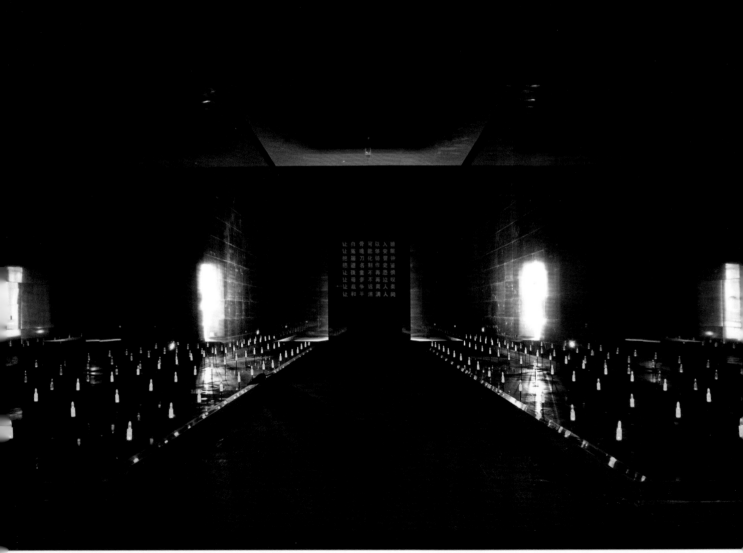

让 白 骨 可 以 入
让 孤 魂 能 都 安
把 罹 道 刀 够 定
绝 难 名 剁 铸 钟
让 孤 童 梦 不 作
让 每 童 梦 不 再
一 让 战 争 远 离
让 和 平 洒 满

The Peace Park 8

The colour green represents life. The Peace Park is composed of green turf, shrubs, tall trees such as cedars, whitebark pines, ginkgos and metasequoias, and a 160-metre-long pond faced with black granite, creating an atmosphere of serenity and vitality. The shadows of the Meditation Hall and the Wall of Victory projected onto the pond surface as clear as a huge mirror seem to shed light on the past, while the green groves, meadows, blue sky and white clouds symbolize a peaceful today and hopeful tomorrow.

1 The Lawn in the Peace Park **2** The Pond in the Peace Park

1

2

The Memorial Hall of the Victims in Nanjing Massacre by Japanese Invaders

Part III. **Sculptures**

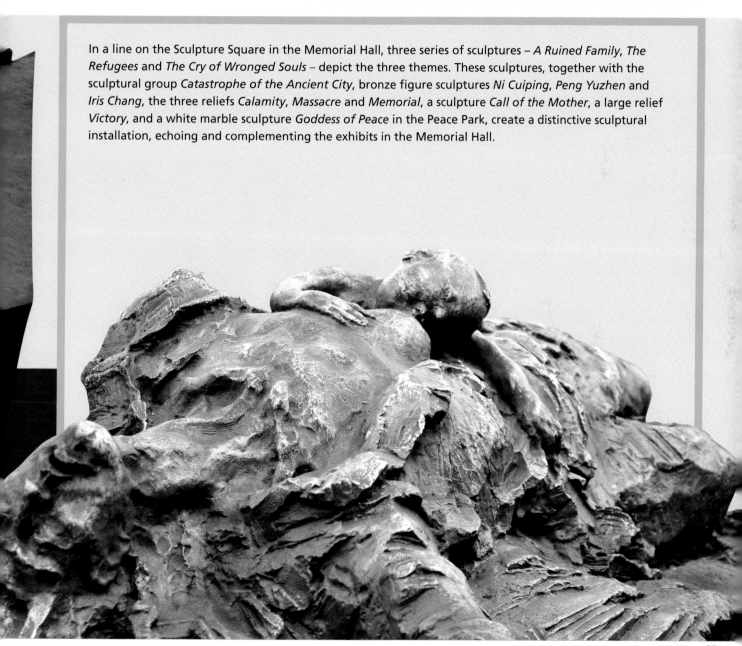

In a line on the Sculpture Square in the Memorial Hall, three series of sculptures – *A Ruined Family*, *The Refugees* and *The Cry of Wronged Souls* – depict the three themes. These sculptures, together with the sculptural group *Catastrophe of the Ancient City*, bronze figure sculptures *Ni Cuiping*, *Peng Yuzhen* and *Iris Chang*, the three reliefs *Calamity*, *Massacre* and *Memorial*, a sculpture *Call of the Mother*, a large relief *Victory*, and a white marble sculpture *Goddess of Peace* in the Peace Park, create a distinctive sculptural installation, echoing and complementing the exhibits in the Memorial Hall.

1 The Sculpture Square

A Ruined Family, *The Refugees* and *The Cry of Wronged Souls* were made in 2007 by Wu Weishan, President of China Sculpture Academy and Professor of Nanjing University. These series of sculptures, all based on the history of the Nanjing Massacre, bring to life the atrocities committed by the Japanese Army in Nanjing in both a realistic and symbolic manner. As a prelude to the theme of the Memorial Hall, these sculptures will tug at visitors' heartstrings.

A Ruined Family

The eye-catching *A Ruined Family*, 12.13 metres high, depicts a heartbroken mother holding her dead child in her arms, uttering heart-rending cries. This sculpture conveys the depth of the humiliation and suffering the Chinese nation has undergone.

A Ruined Family
Wu Weishan

The Memorial Hall of the Victims in Nanjing Massacre by Japanese Invaders

The Refugees

The Refugees, comprising a set of 10 bronze sculptures, portrays a group of refugees including a grief-ridden civilian, a dying couple and a pregnant woman. Placed in a pond, the sculpture embodies the terrible distress of thousands of victimized families.

The Refugees
Wu Weishan

悲愤的飞机又来轰炸了……
失去双亲的孤儿，
在喜鲁的杀声里，
在尸横遍地的巷道里，
在已经麻木了的惊吓与恐惧里……

The devils have sent the bombers again...
The poor orphans,
Frightened by the vicious laugh of the brutal devils,
Terrified by the corpses piling up in the alley,
Have lapsed into numbness...

逃啊！　　　　Run!

The Cry of Wronged Souls

Integrating two abstract sculptures, *The Cry of Wronged Souls* is carved with 'crying figures' in relief on two large angular stones, implying the wrongs, cries, struggles and protests of numerous souls.

The Cry of Wronged Souls
Wu Weishan

1

Catastrophe of the Ancient City is composed of single sculptures, such as the *Broken City Wall*, the *Damaged Sabre*, *Bridge of History*, *Head of a Victim* and *Arm of a Victim* as well as pebble stones symbolic of the remains of the victims. The implied significance of such group sculpture reflects the theme of 'Grief and Indignation'.

1 The Cenotaph is engraved with the date of Nanjing Massacre – 13 December 1937 to January 1938
2 *Catastrophe of the Ancient City*, Qi Kang and Wu Xianlin

2

1 Head of a Victim
2 Arm of a Victim
3 *The Footprints of Historical Witnesses* comprises a road of footprints cast in bronze of the 222 survivors of the Nanjing Massacre and members of the International Military Tribunal for the Far East
The stone tablet wall bearing the name of the Memorial Hall inscribed by Deng Xiaoping

1

2

4

3

The Memorial Hall of the Victims in Nanjing Massacre by Japanese Invaders

1 Bronze sculptures of survivors of Nanjing Massacre: *Ni Cuiping* (at the front) and *Peng Yuzhen*
  Wu Xianlin

2 This is a sculpture by Wang Hongzhi of Iris Chang, a Chinese-American female writer. Her book *The Rape of Nanking: The Forgotten Holocaust of World War II* has enabled people in the USA and elsewhere in the West to learn about the history of the Nanjing Massacre. Tragically, she committed suicide due to her depression in 2004. Facing visitors the sculpture stands opposite the sculptures of the survivors, implying that the survivors give testimony to the history of the Nanjing Massacre in the East while Iris Chang explains this history for people in the West.

2

The Memorial Hall of the Victims in Nanjing Massacre by Japanese Invaders

Calamity
Qian Dajing and others

The Memorial Hall of the Victims in Nanjing Massacre by Japanese Invaders

Memorial
Qian Dajing and others

Massacre
Qian Dajing and others

Wall Bearing the Names of the Victims of the Nanjing Massacre

The *Wall Bearing the Names of the Victims of the Nanjing Massacre*, 43 metres long and 3.5 metres high, is made of granite. Called the 'Wailing Wall' by local people, the Wall is carved with over 10,000 names of the victims of the Nanjing Massacre, a small fraction of the over 300,000 victims in total.

Based on film footage shot by John Magee, an American missionary who was in Nanjing during the massacre, the sculpture depicts an old woman with a bamboo stick in her hand searching for her family members. Overcome with grief, she holds out her left hand as if she were calling and looking for her lost family members.

Victory, 140-metre long sculpture in relief, extends to both sides in the form of the letter 'V' in a token of victory, expressing the elation of the Chinese people for the victory in the War Against Japanese.

Victory Wu Weishan

9 Goddess of Peace

A visit to the Memorial Hall ends at the white marble sculpture *Goddess of Peace*, the last sculpture of the display. Completed in September 2008, the sculpture comprises a mother with a dove of peace in her hand and a child, giving voice to people's anticipation for peace. The sculpture is 30 metres high, in memory of the over 300,000 compatriots slaughtered in the Nanjing Massacre.

1

1 The Peace Park
2 The white marble sculpture *Goddess of Peace*
  Sun Jiabin

2

Since 1985, the Nanjing Municipal Government has set up 17 monuments in memory of the victims of the Nanjing Massacre at the site of the burial ground. In addition, Japanese friends and local residents have erected five more monuments, hence a total of 22, of which 19 are depicted here.

1

2

3

4

5

6

7

8

9

1 Monument to the Victims Slaughtered at Zhengjue Temple
2 Monument to the Victims Slaughtered at Pude Temple
3 Monument to the Victims Slaughtered on Mount Wutai
4 Monument to the Victims Slaughtered at Caoxie Gorge
5 Monument to the Victims Slaughtered at Beiji Pavilion
6 Monument to the Victims Slaughtered at Zhongshan Dock
7 Monument to the Victims Slaughtered on Mount Qingliang
8 Monument to the Victims Slaughtered at the University of Nanjing
9 Monument to the Victims Slaughtered at Stork Gate

1

3

4

5

2

6

8

9

7

10

1 Monument to the Victims Slaughtered at Huashen Temple
2 Monument to the Victims Slaughtered at Jiangdongmen
3 Monument to the Victims Slaughtered at Taiping Gate
4 Monument to the Victims Slaughtered at Hanzhongmen
5 Monument to the Victims Slaughtered in the Eastern Suburb of Nanjing
6 Monument to the Victims Slaughtered at Shangxinhe
7 Monument to the Victims Slaughtered at the Swallow Promontory
8 Monument to the Victims Slaughtered at the Coal Harbour
9 Monument to the Victims Slaughtered at the Xiaguan Power Plant
10 Monument to the Victims Slaughtered at Yijiangmen

The Memorial Hall of the Victims in Nanjing Massacre by Japanese Invaders

Part IV. **Commemorative Events**

As a public cultural facility, the Memorial Hall enables people to pay homage to the victims of the Nanjing Massacre and to voice their sorrow. As well, it organizes academic studies on the history of the Nanjing Massacre and carries out commemorative events both at home and abroad in order to oppose aggressive wars and safeguard world peace.

1 Since 1994, a special ceremony has been held in commemoration of the victims of the Nanjing Massacre on 13 December every year in Nanjing, where sirens are sounded and peace doves are released to urge people not to forget history.

2 Carrying a candle in cupped hands, medical workers in Nanjing grieve over the victims of the Nanjing Massacre

3 The Memorial Ceremony with Candlelight for the Victims of the Nanjing Massacre

4 Religious communities from France, Japan and other countries visiting the Memorial Hall to say prayers for the victims of the Nanjing Massacre

5 Monks in both China and Japan hold a religious assembly for the victims of the Nanjing Massacre every year to pray for peace

6 In 1987, a mission to China from the Commonwealth of Nations paid homage to the victims of the Nanjing Massacre in the Memorial Hall

6

7

8

9

10

11

7 On 17 September 1995, an Israeli Parliamentary mission to China was photographed in the Memorial Hall

8 On 13 September 1996, James Schlesinger, former US Secretary of Defense, visited the Memorial Hall, leaving his comment, 'This is a shocking and tragic historical event beyond compare, and very instructive

9 On 6 May 1998, Margaret Reid, President of the Australian Senate, visited the Memorial Hall

10 On 12 October 2001, Kang Young-Hoon, former Prime Minister of the Republic of Korea, together with his entourage visited the Memorial Hall

11 On 24 May 1998, Tomiichi Murayama, former Prime Minister of Japan, together with his entourage visited the Memorial Hall

1 On 19 August 2001, Toshiki Kaifu, former Prime Minister of Japan, together with his entourage visited the Memorial Hall and made an inscription

2 Young people line up at the entrance to visit the Memorial Hall

3 On 13 September 2003, Johannes Rau, former German President, met two of the survivors of the Nanjing Massacre – Mu Xifu and Li Shizhen, a couple who were protected by John H. D. Rabe

4 Takako Doi, Chairperson of Social Socialist Party and Speaker of the House of Representatives of Japan, laid a wreath in memory of the victims of the Nanjing Massacre

5

6

7

8

9

10

5 The Japan–China Friendship Association in Japan sends a mission to visit the Memorial Hall every spring to atone for the war crimes of the Japanese Army in the form of tree planting, which is regarded as 'Green Expiation'. So far, the event has continued for over two decades.

6 Japanese high school students visited the Memorial Hall to pay homage to the victims of the Nanjing Massacre

7 The 'Eternal Remembrance Association' in Japan visits the Memorial Hall on 15 August (on 15 August 1945 Emperor Hirohito declared the surrender of Japan) every year to express its wishes of remembering forever the victims, opposing wars and praying for peace.

8 On 17 October 1996, a mission sent by the New Production Troupe in Japan to China visited the Memorial Hall, kneeling in tribute to the remains of the victims

9 The Memorial Hall held more than 10 temporary exhibitions including *Exhibition of the Historical Records of the Jews Slaughtered by the Germans* and *Exhibition of Literature on John H. D. Rabe*. On 13 August 2000, an exhibition of oil paintings by Japanese painter Shiego Kamada, *Memories of the 20th Century – Auschwitz–Nanjing*, was opened in the Memorial Hall.

10 On 18 April 2009, the exhibition *The Elder Generation's War* from the Philippines was inaugurated in the Memorial Hall. The photo shows the site of the opening ceremony.

1 The Memorial Hall has held an exhibition of historical records of the atrocities of the Nanjing Massacre in over 20 cities nationwide, attended by over a million visitors. This photo shows young people appreciating the exhibition in Beijing.

2 Since 1995, an exhibition of historical records of the atrocities of the Nanjing Massacre has been held in over 20 cities in Denmark, the USA, Italy, the Philippines and Japan. The photo shows the layout of the exhibition in Manila, the Philippines, in November 2009.

3 The Memorial Hall solicited material on the Nanjing Massacre in Japan, the USA, Britain, Germany and Denmark. The picture shows that on 9 December 2004, Zhu Chengshan, Curator of the Memorial Hall, went to Hawaii to interview Fred Riggs, son of Charles Riggs, a member of the International Committee for the Nanking Safety Zone.

4 In December 2001, the Memorial Hall held a ceremony at St Mary's Cathedral in San Francisco, USA, where Catholics, Jews, Christians, Islamists and Buddhists said prayers for the victims of the Nanjing Massacre. TV stations ABC, NBC, CBS and other American mainstream media gave wide publicity to this event, attracting widespread attention in the USA.

5

6

7

5 Around 15 August every year, the Memorial Hall invites experts both at home and abroad to attend a conference of historical studies on the Nanjing Massacre so as to conduct academic exchange in an extensive and profound manner. The picture shows that from 14 to 16 August 1997, over 140 scholars from China, the USA, Germany, Japan and other countries attended the first International Academic Symposium on the History of the Nanjing Massacre Committed by the Japanese Army, held in Nanjing.

6 On 28 March 2002, the first China–Japan–Republic of Korea Forum on Historical Awareness and Peace in East Asia, organized jointly by the Memorial Hall and others concerned was opened in the Nanjing International Convention Centre, where scholars from the three countries jointly initiated the compilation of a history reader *Modern and Contemporary History of Three East Asian Countries*.

7 The Memorial Hall has edited and published a series of books, photo albums and e-publications on the Nanjing Massacre both at home and abroad.

Editor in Chief: Zhu Cheng Shan
Deputy Editor in Chief: Wang Wei Min, Chen Jun Feng and Hou Shu Guang
Text: Zhu Cheng Shan and Liu Yan Jun
Coordinators: Cui Jing and Antony White
Chinese Editor: Yang Ting
English Translation: Antony White and Wang Chen
English Editor: Julie Pickard
Design: Yuan Yin Chang, Li Jing and Xia Wei

ISBN: 978-7-80204-635-1
First published in 2010 by Chang Zheng Publishers

Text and all images except as below
©2010 The Memorial Hall of the Victims in Nanjing Massacre by Japanese Invaders

Images ©2010 Yuan Yinchang
pp2–3, p9, p16 image 3, p43 background, pp56–57 top right and bottom, p67, p70 image 1,
p73, p88, p89 top right and background

This edition ©2010 London Editions (HK) Ltd

The Memorial Hall of the Victims in Nanjing Massacre by Japanese Invaders
In collaboration with London Editions (HK) Ltd

Distributed worldwide outside China by
Scala Publishers Limited
Northburgh House,
10 Northburgh Street,
London EC1V 0AT
United Kingdom
Tel: 44 (0) 207 490 9900

All rights reserved. No part of this book may be reproduced, stored in a retrieval system or transmitted
in any former by any means electronic, mechanical, photocopying, recording or otherwise, without the
written permission of both The Memorial Hall of the Victims in Nanjing Massacre by Japanese Invaders
and London Editions (HK) Ltd.

图书在版编目（ＣＩＰ）数据

侵华日军南京大屠杀遇难同胞纪念馆 ：英文 / 朱成
山主编． — 北京 ：长征出版社，2010.11
　　ISBN 978－7－80204－635－1

　　Ⅰ．①侵… Ⅱ．①朱… Ⅲ．①南京大屠杀－纪念馆－
画册 Ⅳ．① G268.1－64

中国版本图书馆 CIP 数据核字（2010）第 218759 号